THE BEGINNER'S GUIDE
TO   TIKTOK

From Setting Up Your Account to

Going Viral

LINDA SELVIDGE

TABLE OF CONTENT

BONUS

INTRODUCTION

Are you ready to join the TikTok craze and start creating your own viral videos? Look no further. This book, The Beginner's Guide to TikTok: From Setting Up Your Account to Going Viral, is here to give you the tools and knowledge you need to succeed on the platform.

In this comprehensive guide, we will walk you through the basics of setting up your TikTok account and profile, finding and using popular hashtags, and creating engaging and shareable content. We'll also provide tips and tricks for growing your following and maximizing your reach on the platform.

But that's not all! We'll also delve into the secrets of going viral on TikTok, with advice on how to create the types of videos that are most likely to be shared and liked by users. Whether you're a complete TikTok newcomer or just looking to up your game, this book has something for you.

So let's get started! With "The Beginner's Guide to TikTok," you'll be well on your way to TikTok fame in no time.

Chapter 1

Understanding the Platform and Its Features

TikTok is a social media platform that allows users to create and share short-form videos, ranging from genres like dance, comedy, and education, that have a duration from 15 seconds to one minute three minutes for some users. TikTok is an international version of Douyin, which was originally released in the Chinese market in September 2016. Since its launch, TikTok Douyin rapidly gained popularity in East Asia, South Asia, Southeast Asia, the United States, Turkey, Russia, and other parts of the world.

One of the unique features of TikTok is its use of music and other licensed content in the videos. Many TikTok users create videos set to popular songs, which has helped to increase the platform's popularity and boost the careers of some music artists. TikTok also offers a range of special effects and filters that users can apply to their videos to make them more visually appealing.

In addition to creating and sharing videos, TikTok users can also engage with other users' content by liking, commenting, and sharing their videos. They can also participate in TikTok's duet feature, which allows them to create a split-screen video that combines their own content with someone else's.

TikTok is available as a free download for iOS and Android devices, and can be accessed through the app or on the web. The app is available in over 150 markets, and is available in over 40 languages.

Overall, TikTok is a fun and creative platform that allows users to express themselves through short-form videos and connect with others around the world. In the following chapters, we will delve deeper into the various features of the platform and provide tips on how to make the most of your TikTok experience.

Chapter 2

Setting Up Your TikTok Account and Profile

Before you can start creating and sharing videos on TikTok, you'll need to set up your account and profile. Here's a step-by-step guide on how to do it:

- Download the TikTok app from the App Store or Google Play Store.
- Open the app and tap the "Sign Up" button.
- Enter your phone number or email address to create an account. You can also sign up using your Facebook or Google account.

- Follow the prompts to create a password and confirm your email address or phone number.
- Once your account is set up, tap the Me icon in the bottom right corner of the screen to access your profile.
- From your profile, you can edit your profile photo, name, and other personal information. You can also link your TikTok account to your Instagram or other social media accounts.
- To make your profile more visible to other users, be sure to include a profile photo and a brief bio that describes your interests and content.
- You can also customize the privacy settings on your account to control who

can see your content and interact with you on the platform.

- Your TikTok profile is your public face on the platform, so take the time to make it represent you and your content. With a well-organized and engaging profile, you'll be more likely to attract followers and build your presence on the platform.

Chapters 3

Creating and Editing Videos: Tips and Tricks

Now that you have a TikTok account and profile set up, it's time to start creating and sharing your own videos! Here are some tips and tricks to help you get started:

Choose your topic or theme: Before you start filming, think about what you want to create a video about. It could be a specific subject, such as a hobby or talent, or a particular theme, like comedy or dance.

Find the right music: Music is a key component of many TikTok videos, so take the time to find the right song or sound to set the tone for your video. TikTok has a wide range of licensed music that you can use for your videos, or you can upload your own audio.

Film and edit your video: Once you have your topic and music selected, it's time to start filming. TikTok has a range of camera and editing tools that you can use to create professional-looking videos. You can also use the app's special effects and filters to enhance the visuals of your video.

Add captions and effects: Captions can help to add context to your video and make it more engaging for viewers. TikTok also offers a range of text and graphic effects that you can use to add visual interest to your video.

Share your video: When your video is complete, it's time to share it with the TikTok community. You can post your video to your profile and use hashtags and challenges to increase its visibility on the platform.

With these tips and tricks, you'll be well on your way to creating engaging and shareable TikTok videos. Keep experimenting and have fun!

Chapter 4

Using Hashtags and Discovering Popular Content

Hashtags are a key component of TikTok's discoverability features, and can help to increase the visibility and engagement of your videos. Here's how to use hashtags on the platform:

Find relevant hashtags: Before you start using hashtags, take the time to research popular and relevant hashtags for your content. You can do this by looking at the hashtags used by other creators in your niche, or by using TikTok's search function to find popular hashtags.

Use a mix of popular and niche hashtags: While it's important to use popular hashtags to increase the reach of your videos, it's also a good idea to use more specific, niche hashtags to reach a targeted audience.

Use hashtags in your captions and comments: In addition to using hashtags in your video captions, you can also use them in the comments section of your own and other users' videos. This can help to increase the visibility of your content and expose it to a wider audience.

Follow and engage with users and hashtags: One of the best ways to increase your visibility on TikTok is to engage with other users and their content. Follow users and hashtags that are relevant to your interests, and like and comment on their videos to increase your chances of being discovered by new followers.

By using hashtags effectively and engaging with the TikTok community, you can increase the reach and engagement of your content and build your following on the platform.

Chapter 5

Building Your Following: Engaging with Other Users and Collaborating with Creators

One of the keys to success on TikTok is building a strong and engaged following. Here are some strategies for increasing your followers and engaging with other users on the platform:

- **Post consistently:** To keep your followers interested and engaged, it's important to post new content regularly. Aim to post at least a few times a week to maintain your presence on the platform.

Use hashtags and participate in challenges: Hashtags and challenges are a great way to increase the visibility of your content and attract new followers. Find popular hashtags and challenges that are relevant to your content, and use them to get your videos in front of a larger audience.

Engage with your followers and other users: Interacting with your followers and other users on TikTok is a crucial part of building a strong community. Like and comment on their videos, and respond to comments on your own content to show that you value your followers and are interested in their opinions.

Collaborate with other creators: Collaborating with other creators on TikTok can be a great way to expand your reach and build relationships within the community. Look for creators who produce content similar to your own, and reach out to them about the possibility of doing a collaboration.

By following these strategies and consistently engaging with your followers and other users, you can build a strong and loyal following on TikTok.

Chapter 6

Going Viral on TikTok: Strategies for Creating Shareable Content

While going viral on TikTok is largely a matter of luck, there are certain strategies that you can follow to increase the chances of your content being shared and reaching a wider audience. Here are some tips for creating shareable content on the platform:

Use popular music and sounds: One of the keys to going viral on TikTok is using popular music and sounds in your videos. Look for songs and sounds that are currently trending on the platform, and use them in your content to increase its chances of being shared.

Participate in challenges: Challenges are a great way to get your content in front of a large audience and potentially go viral. Find challenges that are relevant to your content and participate in them to increase the chances of your videos being shared.

Create visually appealing content: TikTok users are more likely to share videos that are visually appealing and well-produced. Use the app's camera and editing tools to create professional-looking videos, and apply special effects and filters to enhance their visual appeal.

Tell a story: Videos that tell a story or convey an emotional message are often more likely to be shared on TikTok. Think about how you can use your content to tell a compelling story or convey a message that will resonate with your audience.

By following these strategies and consistently creating shareable content, you can increase your chances of going viral on TikTok. Remember, however, that going viral is largely a matter of luck, so don't get discouraged if your content doesn't take off right away. Keep experimenting and have fun!

Chapter 7

Maximizing Your Reach and Monetizing Your Videos

Once you have built a following on TikTok and are consistently creating shareable content, you may be interested in maximizing your reach on the platform and monetizing your videos. Here are some strategies for achieving these goals:

Use paid promotion: TikTok offers a range of paid promotion options that can help to increase the visibility of your content. These options include sponsored hashtags, challenges, and ads. By using paid promotion, you can target your content to specific audiences and increase the chances of it being seen by more people.

Collaborate with brands: Brands are increasingly turning to TikTok influencers to promote their products and services. If you have a large following on the platform, you may be able to collaborate with brands on sponsored content and other promotional campaigns.

Monetize your content: TikTok offers a monetization program for eligible creators that allows them to earn money from their content. To be eligible for the program, you must have a large following and consistently create high-quality content.

By following these strategies and consistently creating shareable content, you can increase your reach and monetize your TikTok videos. Remember to always follow the platform's terms of service and guidelines when promoting content or collaborating with brands.

Chapter 8

Conclusion: Continuing Your TikTok Journey

Congratulations on completing The Beginner's Guide to TikTok From Setting Up Your Account to Going Viral. We hope that you've found this guide helpful and that you feel more confident about using the platform to create and share your own videos.

As you continue your TikTok journey, remember to have fun and experiment with different types of content. Keep an eye on the trends and popular hashtags, and don't be afraid to try new things.

Remember that building a following on TikTok takes time and consistent effort, so don't get discouraged if your content doesn't take off right away. Keep creating and sharing high-quality content, and you'll eventually see your following grow.

Finally, don't forget to engage with your followers and other users on the platform. Building relationships and being a part of the TikTok community is an important part of the experience.

We hope that you continue to enjoy using TikTok and that it becomes a fun and rewarding platform for you. Good luck on your journey!

BONUS

Discover these amazing tips that will help your garden go viral on TikTok!

Unveiling the Secrets: How to Make Your Garden Go Viral on TikTok!

In today's digital age, TikTok has emerged as a powerful platform for sharing creative and inspiring content. From dance challenges to DIY hacks, TikTok has become a hub for creators to showcase their talents and passions. Now, gardening enthusiasts can also leverage the platform's immense reach and captivate a global audience with their beautiful gardens! If you've been dreaming of your garden gaining fame on TikTok, then look no further. We've compiled a comprehensive guide filled with amazing tips that will undoubtedly make your garden go viral on TikTok! Get ready to unveil the hidden secrets and watch your garden flourish on this mesmerizing platform.

1. Create Stunning Visuals:

The key to capturing TikTok users' attention lies in producing visually captivating content. Invest time in setting up your garden in a picturesque manner. Use strategic lighting during different times of the day to create striking contrasts. Focus on presenting the unique features of your plants, flowers, and landscaping elements in a way that leaves viewers in awe. Play with angles and add some artistic flair to your videos to make them stand out from the crowd.

2. Tell a Compelling Story:

People love stories that evoke emotions and inspire them. Share your gardening journey on TikTok in a compelling way. Highlight the challenges you've overcome, your successes, and even your failures, and showcase how your garden has transformed over time. A relatable and heartfelt narrative will help establish a deeper connection with your audience, making them more likely to follow and engage with your content.

3. Incorporate Time-Lapse Videos:

Time-lapse videos are an absolute favorite on TikTok as they allow viewers to witness the gradual growth and blooming of plants in a matter of seconds. Capture your garden's evolution over days, weeks, or even months and condense it into a mesmerizing time-lapse clip. These bite-sized visual treats are shareable and easily go viral, attracting a broader audience to your gardening journey.

4. Engage with Trending Challenges:

Stay up-to-date with the latest TikTok trends and challenges, and find creative ways to incorporate them into your gardening content. Whether it's a popular dance, a transition effect, or a specific hashtag challenge, adapting these trends to showcase your garden will not only boost your visibility but also increase your chances of reaching a broader demographic.

5. Offer Valuable Gardening Tips:

Educate and inspire your audience by sharing valuable gardening tips and tricks. Whether it's about propagating plants, composting, or maintaining a beautiful garden, providing useful information will position you as an authority in your niche. TikTok users love to learn new things, and by imparting your knowledge, you'll gain a loyal following eager to see more of your content.

6. Collaborate with Other TikTok Creators:

Collaboration is a powerful tool on TikTok. Team up with other gardening enthusiasts, influencers, or even local experts to create exciting content together. Cross-promote each other's videos to tap into each other's audiences and gain new followers. Collaborations add variety to your feed and offer a fresh perspective, making your garden content more engaging and dynamic.

7. Leverage TikTok's Editing Tools:

TikTok's editing tools are designed to enhance creativity. Experiment with filters, effects, text, and music to add an extra layer of charm to your garden videos. But remember, subtlety is key; don't overdo it, as you want your garden to be the star of the show.

Gardening on TikTok is not just about showcasing your beautiful garden; it's about sharing your passion, knowledge, and experiences with the world. By following these amazing tips, you'll have the formula to make your garden go viral on TikTok! Stay consistent, engage with your audience, and let your love for gardening shine through in every video you create. Embrace the power of TikTok, and soon enough, your garden will be the talk of the town, captivating viewers from all corners of the globe. Happy gardening and happy TikToking!

Unleashing the Power of TikTok: 10 Marketing Tips to Skyrocket Your Brand

In the ever-evolving landscape of digital marketing, TikTok has emerged as a formidable platform that captures the hearts and minds of millions. With its engaging short-form videos and a diverse user base, TikTok presents a golden opportunity for businesses to connect with their target audience and drive brand awareness. To help you harness the full potential of this dynamic platform, we have curated 10 marketing tips that will elevate your TikTok game and propel your brand to new heights:

1. Embrace Authenticity: TikTok thrives on authentic and genuine content. Show the human side of your brand by crafting videos that evoke emotions, tell stories, and connect with users on a personal level. Avoid overly polished content; instead, focus on being relatable and real to build trust and loyalty.

2. Master the Art of Storytelling: Compelling storytelling is the secret ingredient to capturing TikTok users' attention. Create narratives that resonate with your target audience, using relatable characters and a clear beginning, middle, and end. A well-told story will leave a lasting impression and keep viewers coming back for more.

3. Leverage Trends Creatively: Stay on top of TikTok trends and challenges, and don't be afraid to join the fun! Participating in trending challenges can boost your visibility and reach a wider audience. Add a unique twist that aligns with your brand to make your content stand out from the crowd.

4. Keep it Short and Sweet: TikTok's magic lies in its short-form video format, so keep your content concise and to the point. Aim for videos that are 15 to 60 seconds long, delivering your message efficiently and leaving viewers wanting more.

5. Engage with your Audience: Engagement is key to building a loyal following. Respond to comments, address questions, and acknowledge user-generated content featuring your brand. Building a sense of community around your brand will encourage user loyalty and advocacy.

6. Collaborate with Influencers: Influencers hold immense sway over TikTok's audience. Partnering with relevant influencers can expose your brand to a broader set of followers and lend credibility to your products or services. Choose influencers whose values align with your brand to ensure authentic collaborations.

7. Utilize Hashtags Strategically: Hashtags play a vital role in content discovery on TikTok. Research trending and relevant hashtags within your niche and incorporate them into your videos. Develop a branded hashtag to encourage user-generated content and foster a sense of belonging.

8. Showcase Behind-the-Scenes Content: TikTok users crave a peek behind the curtain. Offer glimpses of your team, product development, or the making of your content. Humanizing your brand through behind-the-scenes videos will deepen your audience's connection with your brand.

9. Drive Traffic with CTAs: Encourage your audience to take action by using clear and compelling calls-to-action (CTAs). Whether it's to visit your website, subscribe to your newsletter, or try out a product, direct viewers on what steps to take next.

10. Analyze and Optimize: Finally, always track the performance of your TikTok marketing efforts. Use TikTok's analytics to gauge the success of your campaigns, identify what content resonates best with your audience, and make data-driven decisions to refine your strategy continually.

Incorporate these 10 marketing tips into your TikTok strategy, and you'll unlock the potential to reach millions of engaged users, propel your brand to new heights, and establish lasting connections with your target audience. TikTok is a dynamic and ever-changing platform, so stay agile, creative, and authentic to stand out in this exciting digital landscape. Happy TikToking!